Other books by the author:

POETRY
The Stone Spiral (Giant Steps, 1987, reprinted 1988)
Ten Letters to John Muir (Burbage Books, 1990)
Outcrops (Littlewood/Arc, 1991)
The Rope (Redbeck Press, 1996)
The Blue Bang Theory: New Nature Poetry (with John Sewell,
        Colin Sutherill and Diana Syder, Redbeck Press, 1997)
Whale Watching with a Boy and a Goat (Redbeck Press, 1998)

CRITICISM
Ted Hughes: A Critical Study (with Neil Roberts, Faber and Faber,
                                                                    1981)
Green Voices: Understanding Contemporary Nature Poetry
                                    (Manchester University Press, 1995)
The New Critical Idiom: Pastoral (Routledge, 1999)

EDUCATION
Teaching A Level English Literature: A Student-Centred Approach
                                    (with John Brown, Routledge, 1989)

EDITING
John Muir: The Eight Wilderness-Discovery Books (Diadem, 1992)
Not Not Not Not Not Enough Oxygen and Other Plays by Caryl
                                    Churchill (with Gill Round, Longman, 1993)
Orogenic Zones: The First Five Years of the International Festival of
                                    Mountaineering Literature (with Rosie Smith,
                                                                    Bretton Hall, 1994)
John Muir: His Life and Letters and Other Writings (Bâton Wicks,
                                                                    1996)
The Climbers' Club Centenary Journal (Climbers' Club, 1997)
The Literature of Nature: An International Sourcebook (UK chapters,
                                    with Patrick Murphy, Fitzroy Dearborn, 1998)

THE UNRELIABLE MUSHROOMS
NEW AND SELECTED POEMS

Terry Gifford

2003

The Unreliable Mushrooms: New and Selected Poems
is published by Redbeck Press, 24 Aireville Road,
Frizinghall, Bradford, BD9 4HH.

Art and design by Russell Mills, based on his work
'Fall to Rise' (see p. 96).
Print by Arc & Throstle Press, Nanholme Mill
Shaw Wood Road, Todmorden, Lancs. OL14 6DA.

The Unreliable Mushrooms: New and Selected Poems
ISBN 1 904338 02 X

Redbeck Press acknowledges financial assistance
from the Arts Council of England, Yorkshire.

Acknowledgements are due to the following magazines,
journals and books, in which some of these poems were
first published: Giants Steps: *The Stone Spiral*, 1987
(reprinted in 1988); Littlewood Arc: *Outcrops*, 1991;
Redbeck Press: *The Rope*, 1996, and *Whale Watching with
a Boy and a Goat*, 1998; 'English Earth Warriors' was
published in *ISLE* (USA); 'A Milesian Encounter with a
Spider in Spain' was read on 'Arts Today', Australian
Broadcasting Company; 'The Charcoal Burner's Tale' was
published in *The Reader*; 'Cretan Post-Pastoral' was
published in *PAN* (Australia).

For John Sewell and Diana Syder
for help with this selection

and also for
Elizabeth Barrett, Kevin Borman, David Duncombe
and Colin Sutherill with thanks for the monthly
feedback over all these years.

CONTENTS

The Stone Spiral (1987)

Outcrops (1991)

The Rope (1996)

Whale Watching with a Boy and a Goat (1998)

The Unreliable Mushrooms: New Poems

THE STONE SPIRAL (1987)

Water Powers
for David Craig

Refuelling from the meres of Leighton Moss
The migrating osprey waits for fish.
Next meals are from the seas off Africa.

We're powered by a nuclear fission
And visit water's equinoctial force
As tourists, turning from Heysham Power Station
To watch the tide beside Victorian railway arches
Over the Kent, where the upsurging sea
Bottles into the bridged neck of the river.

Drawn together, expectant, half-anxious here
With the children at the edge, we wait,
Daring the water powers to swirl their worst
At our feet. A hooter cranks across empty sands
And we strain to sense a bore race
White in the distance like a rolling rope.
Slowly it comes against the wind-whipped river,
Chuckles, chewing at the bones of the bridge.

But up from the sea over the river
Races the rain, instantly draining russet fells
To winter grey, forcing us up for shelter
Between rising water and iron rails.
As river, sea and rain close,
Last lightning strikes the summer,
Thunder splits the seasons,
A train leaps into the vortex
Over our heads, under our skulls.
'Nuclear waste,' you say,
'They're sometimes carrying –
Black canisters of concrete
For rolling simply into the sea!'

Fish, osprey and all of us must wait
For what the seasons' chains will carry
When water powers work their worst
On our advanced naivities.

Whale Cry

I hear you, blue whale
Mewing like a buzzard,
Your sad questions rising
Through the sound waves softly
And I cannot answer.

Baleen? Baleen?
Your questions echo
Through the bone
Of your trawl-teeth bristles.
Brushes and bendy stays were
Absurd answers to your firm demise.

Oil? Oil? Oil?
Your questions bubble to the light
Of our electric age, tuned
One way, guiltily silent
To explain 'Fertiliser' or 'Cosmetics'
To your slow extinction.

Largest living marvel of the planet
Your deep intelligence knows I hear
And turns back under the ice
Flying slowly through the blue,
Calling, and I cannot answer.

The Stone Spiral

It squats in stone
Buddha-like, biding its time,
Accepting its own nature,
Its ribbed shell now
A spiral of white arches
Settled into the flat planes
Of sea-sediment stone.

An ammonite in Freiburg
Decorates a window ledge –
Borrowed time for a smart flat.
The trees of the Black Forest
Fold inwards under each year's
Crop of industrial rainfall.

A glass case in Finale Ligure
Cages a flotsam collection
Of the tiny sea creatures.
The turquoise pool of the Mediterranean
Clouds a little more with the swirls
Of each year's sewage and oil.

Even here in Provence
Where aromas rise on the thermals
Under the white heat of Mont St. Victoire
Herbs have been harvesting
Radiation from the rain storms
Spiralling out of Russia.

And as we turn the circle
Of our rock-climbing journey towards
Home and names of sites for locking
Time-bombs of waste in rain-tight rock
I wonder by what form – bunker or core,
A menhir or a Henry Moore – our species
Will be known to its inheritors.

Living at the Limit of their Range

On the last day they looked down on the sea
As planned, two sweaty naturalists crossing the map,
Observers not disturbers of the field, of course.
Recorders of survival, they were not surviving well.
Last water drunk, they flopped onto the barren summit,
Looked back to see deer launching into a lochan,
A herd of longships, prows bending to drink.
Under their boots in the quartz-prismed glare
Sea pink's tissue-paper blooms survived far from the sea.
Midday, white boulders, and weirdly, no island wind.
The mountain shouldered them off. Stumbling wildly
They raced towards the curve of Claggain Bay.

A sea trout leapt in front of them, thick as an arm,
Upright, fisting clear of the water, black-spotted silver
Hung in an alchemical moment of sea, air, and sun.
Field sketch for the record. Then they saw the stalking
Seal. So ecstacies of fear turn fish to air.
But now the Arctic Terns were screeching overhead,
And needed for nest records too, breeding in Britain
At the limit of their range. Icicles of the air,
Squealing on the wavelength of a high pitch of pain,
They bobbed like nervous drips, beaks blood-red, so close
White wings were transparent as silk to the sun.
Noting the two eggs, the taller man was struck
On the scalp. An instant penetration. Covering their heads
In a strange crouching run two creatures were observed
Moving in the direction of walls and roof.

The Sundew's Secret

It is hard to stalk
In a low land, exposed
Not only to an iron wind
But circling horizons
That snare the mind
In the midsummer dusk
After the spirit has been sapped
From the legs by soft peat.

He paused, knowing small eyes
Were upon him in the empty
Wet waste. Bobbins of bogcotton
Nodded his presence. Pink bursts
Of lousewort turned to inspect
His inspection of them. And here
Was another low lochan, fringed
Like a sundew, by rusted fronds.

Directions for a last search
Needed sifting, now he knew
He grew weak. Pushing off again
He sank into black water
Then wrenched out, eyes still
Scanning the lochan's surface.
Half sunken shapes rode out
Through wavelets, beaks sensing air.

The dark russet patch of
The Red Throated Diver gave him
The secret he sought. He drank
Through binoculars, breath held,
All the sensuous details he knew
Would soon take to the sky.
Whiter than bogbean's flower
A breast flashed in the low light.

Suddenly paddles were running
On water and an eel awkwardly
Flew, neck slung low, black feet
Trailing fins. On an island
A basket of grass showed
A dragon-green egg. He turned
In the sundew with his secret
To consider, only now, starting back.

Hen Harrier

Princess of the razor stare
glistening black as her beak,
an edge sliced from a dark sun,
she revolves her thick feathered neck,
sharply silent as the teeth of her necklace,
sensing betrayal on each breeze.
Her wings, her chequered court of the air,
in hiding lie as the slates of her back.
A sudden shriek lifts her
to her black gloved prince,
the white schooner of the sky.
Upturning she grabs his gift.

Castlerigg Stone Circle

'The magic is to make them move.'

From the rigg we looked across a garth
To Skelthwaite above the Naddle Beck
Seeking signs in nicks and grooves

Of an earlier language in the landscape,
Meanings made by silent lines
Of distance from these standing stones.

It was our first conversation.
The wind played freely with your hair
Across your face freckled with rain.

Your voice. The blackthorn hedge. Lifting mists.
The Scots, I said, must have many words
For weather such as this and worse.

We kept trying, inside the cold circle
Of polished shrunken stones
But the heart had gone. Shivers

Made me run to the field bottom, turn,
And walking slowly up I suddenly saw
Teeth rising from the roots of the hill

Speaking a craggy vernacular
Strong and clear, like a shout.
Strong and clear you step free

Of the circle, and as I cross the field
To meet you, the stones too turn
To touch and pass by in the wind.

Dunnerdale 1979

The Duddon is a teeming valley,
A poacher's pocket hidden soft and deep
In the coarse folds of the Cumbrian coat.
Alive with mice, owls and weazles,
Its breathing air hung with hawks,
Torn by stoops of peregrine.

From the huddled shoulder of Bigert Mire
That Easter we watched flocks of
Calling curlew passing overhead
From open estuary
To boggy breeding fells beyond
The headwall of Wallowbarrow Crag.

Turning from the ground-frost
And warm pace of early lambing
The farmer said, 'Tuarts are back!'
Lapwings tumbled from the sky
Above his calving byre,
Miming the birth cries of last night.

I remember I couldn't believe it:
Two buzzards mating on the turf
At Whinfield Ground. Brief
As a sway of the gorse he settled on her
Then lifted, side-slipped,
Soaring to the south.

I remember I stood uncomfortable
Under the lychgate of Ulpha church.
A soaring buzzard suddenly closed,
Fell on Rainsbarrow Wood,
But softly glided up
Out of the oaks.

And there you were, walking embarrassed
From the phone box to tell me
What you'd known as sure as spring:
Our Ruth was growing in Dunnerdale that evening.
Flightless I soared
And sank and soared.

OUTCROPS (1991)

Hutton Roof

Coming together like this, warmly,
Through the spitting gale
To your local outcrop, images rise
Towards me as I climb rock
Slippery with slime like fish's scales.
My fingers fit the puddled prints
Like St. Peter's thumb in the haddock,
This white flesh fifteen feet thick
On the boney spine of England.

Surfacing at the summit I see
The gaping mouths of flounders
Piled flat, no longer flapping
On this fossilised beach,
Storm-washed and dipping
Into seas of wet bracken
Where my daughter's red hood
Submerges like a vivid flower
I do not want to lose.

She's unaware that I'm awash
With choices. I do not name
The surface of my thoughts.
You do not ask.
With this we're both at sea,
Swimming amongst the coral,
Sunk for the winter under
This surging of clouds, this wind
That tears at the exposed bedrock.

Dolphinarium, Phantasialand, Cologne

I don't think you quite understood
At the time what happened to me
As I faced up to Phantasialand.
The plastic Brandenburg Gates
Were the first hoop after the turnstile,
The surging roller coaster high
On your list, love. I just found
This need to read under the trees.

I hoped we'd meet half-way
At the two o'clock display of dolphins.
But when, sitting alone, I missed you,
Lost with the German commentary,
My heart went out to the dolphins
And you, as I watched the pool
And the door between whistles.

How they leapt and surged,
Lifting their lives clean
Out of their element
For all to see and grasp
In a gasp what dolphin means:
An underwater force bottled
In a gleaming skin of grey plastic,
A blue pool and a great room
Of alien echoes and faces in tiers.

Lawrence in Trier

On the coach back the kite cruising
Beside us, turning and turning choices
Of trees on broad wings of ease, shows us
The ragged browns and whites of his breast.

Turning and turning inside the great black
Permanence of Porta Nigra, the Roman gate,
I tell you that inside I'm in turmoil
Thinking of Lawrence's letter to Ernest Weekly
And you, the butterfly on the spiral stairs
In the heart of Trier, Lawrence's Matlock Town,
Held in the deep red arms of the valley.

Turning and turning in the streets of Trier
We hunt Lawrence's hotel, letters in our hands.
'I love you because of your chin',
He wrote to Frieda, waiting for her
To join him in these streets of 'pink explosions'.
The vines on his hills 'like angry hedgehogs'
Are each pruned to a heart turning and
Turning with the years on upright stakes.

Brimfull like the shining river, you say
You feel secure staked in our red earth.
It's not strange how I suffer in spite of this,
Turning over choices as I watch you,
Purple shirted and delicate, walking around
The cold black bulk of Porta Nigra.
Certainly our nights snatched here have been
Richly red as a kite turning softly upon
The rising air of a wood. At least Lawrence,
Waiting in Trier, had made his choice.

Imbolc

She stood waiting in her sheepskin
Looking down the long dipping line
Of the black gritstone edge,
The bowl of its back sifting snow
Under a wind from the east quarter.

The sun had probably set
Behind that snow-dark sky.
She had probably missed him
Passing through the sacred rocks
On separate tracks to the high point.

Walking on to keep warm
She remembered the sun orange
On orange bracken last Hallowe'en
When he first showed her
The high cave, its tunnel and balcony,

First whispered that they be Imbolc wed.
Now the nerve of that amulet charmer
Had probably failed. 'Walk no further!'
She turned. Panting, he threaded through
Boulders of snow, paused. They walked forwards

To kiss the kiss that binds
But knows the changes of the seasons,
The length of a life.
As their heads parted she smiled,
'How short the shaman has left your hair!'

Two crows passed above, silent,
And she hoped that next year
She would not be here for
The walking apart. They could last,
For all his lateness, beyond the trial.

Now, looking back from a place at the edge
He showed her her head profiled in stone,
Pointed nose and delicate mouth facing west.
Together they ran down towards the tribe where
She would light the great Imbolc fire.

North Hill Tor

Suddenly the horses started running
Over the green salt marsh,
As though fire swept down
Through crags and trees
Catching at their tails,
Till some invisible force turned them
Full gallop back over creeks.

The wild rhythm of slapped mud
Echoed up to us on the rock
Roped together to a single flake,
All four, a new family
Feeling our way, in turn,
Up the slab's surface,
Unnerved slightly
By whatever was going on.

On top I saw a peregrine
Fly free across the marsh,
Peering down, in control,
Like the small daughter I'd left,
Setting out her ducks and geese
On her bedroom floor.
And here three shelduck lifted
Like flags, black and white
Toys set up for the game.
As my stepdaughter tussled
To untie herself I pointed out
The buzzard slowly circling
And as the rain fell

I was the only one
Who heard the first cuckoo.

The Elterwater Otters

In dull dawn light I creep
Across the creaking boards, unlock
The heavy hostel door and hunt
The Elterwater otters once again.

Behind me my children sleep alone
Snug as badgers in their bunks,
If they don't wake. In the midge-soft
Heavy morning it's misty across the meadow.

Tensed for what's behind and what's
Before, swiftly but softly I tread
Gravel by the river. Greenslates glisten
Clear as pennies in a wishing-well.

I watch the dipper underwater,
Its needle head sewing together
The seams of the river as I pass.
Hoping they're still not stirring

Behind me, I stare far downstream
For playful splashes round the rocks
In the shallows and suddenly I'm tripped
By a net of tree roots at my feet.

It must have been as I reached the lake,
Saw the kingfisher dive, flash that blue
Fluorescence of oil in the marsh mud,
That they found my bed was empty.

It must have been as I saw that 'fish'
Paddling along the bed of the lake,
Large as a black log just below me,
That they began to hunt the hostel.

Kate Gifford

My upright grandma bent
Finally from seventy years
Over sink, field and floors,
Died in her apron
On the backroom bed.
As she had bent, fallen, and again
Curled inwards slowly
She stiffened
Against the senility of 'a home'.

The homes her working life had gripped
Were only two, wife and widow.
Her husband's death forced her
From fields of flowers
To the terrace in the town.
In those scrubbed houses
Starched with her iron presence
I always tensed with fear,
Grateful for the chocolate
And the front door, the backward step
To where mistaken wrongdoings
Were as natural as growing up.

During a summer stay,
Ten and turbulent,
Sinking into the fantasies
Of the vast feather bed
I was always troubled
By the vagueness of my guilt.
Sunday School, soap and eleven-plus success
Pleased her and my dead grandad,
'Had he been here'.
Always I drew back
From the boney kiss
And its unspoken demands.

Yet talking, nodding, smiling deeply
She held my babies best,
And when we buried her,
Back in the freshly turned
Village soil, I mourned for this
And her unbroken spirit
That even in death demanded
Our long journey
Behind her polished coffin
From street to stubble
And testing Fenland wind.

Autumn Amulet

A gale tears across the Fens
The Fen wind turns white sails
The sails drive the windshaft
The windshaft creaks its cogs
Small cogs still turn my wheel
My wheel is driven by phone calls
Your calls crackle across the sea
The sea will turn our tide
Tides rise to your return
Your return will cause a gale

Fishface

He knew they had to be passed
Like passing a dog
That smells your fear.

Gary's gang smelled his
And they guarded this street
Into which his family had moved.

Gary made the teams
And the mischief
For his scrawny band of littluns.

'Oi! Fishface!'
He kept walking
But mentally he froze.

He knew he had no safe reply.
They had him hooked
And played him down their line.

Now he could not change.
His ears moved like gills
On the face that swam towards him

Every morning in the mirror.

Mrs Ridgeon's Garden

It was not his father's obvious delight,
It was not the fusty smell of stored apples,
It was not even the eight year old's pride
At cycling with dad's forgotten sandwiches
To 'the old lady's' as it was called at home.

It was the stark formality he entered uneasily
Between clipped high hedges, over even gravel,
Beside turf-trimmed weedless borders, he remembered,
And the slowly growing sense that his father's
Mower, shears, hard-grained hands had shaped

This powerful message for the owner, who,
He slowly realised, also owned his dad.

Zinal Rothorn

for John Driskell

Whilst Zinal slept
We moved upon the mountain,

First by torchlight on moraine
Then dawnlight on ice until

Sunlight fired first peaks,
Caught our breath in the sharp

Thin air that distilled
My first start, first season.

It was to be your last.
Strange, that we've both lost

The photographs, as though
Memory through the whisky glass

Between us, years after
Your first illness, was stronger

Years after we moved together
Step in step upon the mountain.

Borrowdale Evolution

And when they turned at last
In the Jaws of Borrowdale and cried
'After the whale, Save the Saxifrage!'
The fenced paths were white stairways
Onto purple fells fertilised for perfection,
Climbing crags were chalk polished
And made safe with BMC bolts,

Fields farmed rare species
Of nearly lost sheep behind
Electric fences sheathed
In Leisure Park green.

And in the Leisure Park office
After many meetings,
Consternations of conferences,
The committee came up with
The Borrowdale Crag Plan:

Upper Falcon Crag to the ornithological interest,
Beth's Buttress to the botanist, refurbishing the ferns,
Castle Crags to the photographer – National View 5003,
Nitting Haws to the scrambler whose guidebook made history,
Shepherd's Crag to the climber who has coughed up the fee.

Now the climber with her National Certificate
Never envies the ornithologist his Borrowdale permit,
And the windsurfer displaying her Derwentwater Disc
Never speaks to the botanist with his SSSIC.
But sometimes a walker with Self-leadership Grade 3
Applies for a day on the Ecological Trail
In triplicate, for next year, if the Geiger count is clear.

THE ROPE (1996)

The Rope

(Espero Sur Central, Puig Campaña, January 1991)

'Your children become your friends
earlier after a divorce.' Tom tying in
between me and my regular partner

warmed that cold start with an unspoken
bonding beyond the boots and the ropes,
the shared knowledge of the knots.

We had climbed into the sun,
Tom snagging his rucksack
traversing under a tree, crying out

momentarily above me, but knowing
that here you have to free yourself.
It is what we have come for, together.

We do not linger on that ledge
on the open face of the mountain.
Grabbing gear, I lead through and up

until stopped by a tree. I tie on
and take in the rope back to Tom.
I do not think of him as my son.

'Climb when you're ready!'
I call, but Norman shouts up
with an edge of accusation,

'Tom's blue rope has come undone!'
I shudder, suddenly feel sick.
He will retie the knot between us

but a gap has widened between me
and my judgement, me and my son.
I must stay closer, check the knots,

climb as a father not as a friend.
Tom comes smiling up, showing no sign
of being other than an open friend.

Falling

It is still the boldest lead
of his life. He was fifteen,
partnered by a boy of fourteen
from the island who had fallen
leading this route last time.
I watched among the boisterous band
of locals rooting for their boy
and mine on Jersey's highest
Pinnacle. I must ask him about it,

the day he fell away from me
finally, leading beyond where
I could follow. I am driving
to pick him up again. It is the season
of the moon rising red
over dark-early fields and fells.
My child is grown now, seeded
on the wind of his own life.

Tom led off up the towering wall
as agile as a gecko. I kept
taking pictures, swallowing my shout
of 'Get some gear in!' as he ran out
his own rope. The route was called
Total Lack of Control. He placed only
three pieces of protection in ninety feet.
But I was proud of his deft creation
of his three-point hanging belay.

The other boy joined him, traversed left
to meet his nemesis at a notched break
in the overhang. He placed protection,
paused, then pulled through first time
to cheers from below. They cruised it.
I kept remembering to breathe and
take pictures. But my film had not wound
on. I had no photos of Tom falling
away from the old tree by not falling.

Montagne Des Agneaux, 1994

A cold bivvi we had of it,
or so I thought. Choosing
to be without a sleeping bag
myself, I took your turning,
crackling in your plastic bag,
to be suffering as I was,
sleeping in snatches. Not so,
you grunted after the alarm
as I force-fed cheese into
the mouth of a beached merman.
Why was I worrying at you
like a father with a newborn
in the very dead of night?

Suddenly other small lights
appeared amongst the boulders
beyond us like the lanterns
of an ancient army rising
out of the earth itself.
As we moved up moonlit moraine
the first of the speechless
shadows overtook us and
bootkicked up the rising snow.
Pulling out crampons, I dropped
the chocolate you offered.
Quietly, by torchlight, you
found it and gave it me again.

Snow steepened. I pointed out
steps up right. Those from the hut
steamed straight on along the line
of fallen stones. Above it,
stepping from snow to scree,
I knocked off a stone, stood
dumb for the word 'Below!'
as the Frenchman beside me

called out in horror. 'Dad,'
you said, 'you should have called!'
It was not (you may say)
satisfactory. I returned
to snow not a moment too soon.

Then at dawn your 'Look at that!'
stopped us as your first alpine
glory glowed on the peaks
of the Pelvoux and the Ecrin
in a slow cascade of gold.
We turned again and cramponed
along an earthy ledge to look
over the Col du Monêtier
into sun and miles of sheer
white snow below and up
the way we have to go.
We photographed each other
grinning and grinning.

At the vertical rock wall
I followed your line past
the roped-up French, and higher,
on the open rocks, you followed
mine until we came upon
a cairn, a crowd and breathless space.
On this first alpine summit
you produced a dram to toast
the view, your girlfriend's parents
who had given you the hipflask,
and perhaps more, our being
equally unfit, equally poised
between your birth, my death.

To Alison
i.m. Dave Cook

I'm at 39,000 feet and it's desperate.
I don't know how to start this poem.
Home is rushing up fast and I rarely
remember dreams long enough to tell,
even this brief Grand Canyon dream.
Should I begin with the evening before,
camping a mile below the earth's rim,
the sun setting down the river's length,
orange ancient walls, surging brown water,
the lightest breeze lifting white leaves?

Or with Dave's smile suddenly popping up
over the rim of Curbar Edge that day
he'd left his jacket on the train
with the club hut key in it, his gentle joke
against my new mountain bike, the woman
below still struggling with his well-placed
protective gear and a weekend away with Dave?

I've avoided starting with the shuddering
moment of disbelief that Dave, lover of rock
and roll, gritstone, politics and all of us
is dead. Now, how can I broach this dream
I'm carrying back from the canyon bottom
that rock-hard night of tired naked rest
when Dave drifted over through the pubcrowd,
a welcomed mocking smile keen to talk? You see
that's all it is, was, this dream –
I was so pleased to see him, that he
was still around in there somewhere,
that I immediately woke up wanting
to tell you, to register this small joy.

Snow Leopard

She sloughed off her rucksack
and stood stilling her heart,

staring fiercely from this last
rise that was her journey's end.

She would take her time now.
Time was what he had given her.

Misted ridges rose like ghosts
towards their tombstone summits.

It was not as she expected –
so vast, so complex, so bright.

In this stark early light
the range was a wall of white

and blue, snow and shadow
that somewhere held him fast

in a slow echo of his fall
towards the glacier snout.

She would have to face the finding
of his axe, perhaps, even

his body resurfacing, some
future climbers' reluctant

photograph that would show
his scarf, perhaps, before they

rolled him into a crevasse
and turned towards their summit.

It had happened to others before.
Here it could not end for her.

Even the ice kept moving.
Even this morning she had seen

before sunrise, on the opposite
bank, a white on white shadow

she had not sought, and even now
dare not give a name.

'Tophet Wall', Graphite on Paper,
Julian Cooper, 1993.

The artist has entered
the dark of the earth
for tools of black rock
to reflect the climbing
of Tophet Wall where all
is angles of air, sheer
facets of light far above
flat fields and Wast Water.

The artist has entered
the plumbago mines under
Seatoller Common, searched
their litany of levels:
Gilbert's Level, Robson's Level,
German's Vein, Jopson's Vein,
Old Men's Stage, Waddy's Pipe,
black holes in a mountain.

The artist has scrabbled
in rain, a hooded crow
clawing, picking, marking
plumbago on paper,
obsessively scavenging
the four hundred year scree-tip
for apothecary's gold:
'It hath divers purposes.'

The artist has chosen
the tools for Tophet Wall,
a rucksack of rocks once
so precious that miners
imported from Augsburg
were strip-searched on that
Borrowdale fellside
each day leaving work.

Now, knowing the mark
each rock makes in his hand,
the artist remakes the climb,
re-enters the inward search
that is a line on a wall,
a mining of surface,
a slow-moving marriage
of heaven and hell

in the swirling play
of the elements high
on the head of Great Gable.
The mind, inside the rock,
outside the body, lost
in the vastness of crag,
shadow and light,
concentrates on the crux.

This Painting

took 3 days, 6 Vesta meals and a 28 mile walk
to make.
It was in black and white (and grey): lead white,
storm black,
on a 6ft by 5ft primed canvas on an alloy frame,
bulldog clipped,
carried on a rucksack rolled up with brushes in a
ski bag.
Two litres of turps sloshed about in the rucksack with
light pegs
for anchoring the whole sail on a heather bank,
a butt,
under the most majestic, neglected, inaccessible crag
in Scotland:
the north-east face of Bienn Lair. Hornblende schist
gleams green,
bristling its beautiful forms: Butterfly Buttress,
The Tooth.
We climbed Wisdom Buttress in the spitting teeth of
a gale:
a shower on the big slab on the overhangs always
to come,
always worrying above, but outflanked on unseen ledges
incut
for the artist's fingers feeling his way up the earth's
hard core
a long way from rescue, a pint, a car, all other oil
painters.
Back up next day at 11, position chosen, charcoal
outline
in the frame, a wild mile of rock reduced to its
incisors.
The painter does not think of commitment, courage,
the risk

of failure on a large scale in big mountains
far out
which the later sunset down Fionn Loch would not
pay for,
nor evening rainbows above the tent and Dubh Loch
because
at 3 o'clock, in a downpour, this painting was washed
away.

Glendalough, County Wicklow

Ronnie Wathen was a shaman.
Only he knew what it was blew
From the mountains of his life
Through his poems and his pipes.

Waking to a bright morning of white houses
circling Dublin Bay, we rolled off the ferry
and into the cloud-clearing hills of Wicklow,
into the raised glacial arms of Glendalough.
We passed St Kevin's sixth century retreat,
its round tower, rounded Celtic crosses,
to walk through the Scots pines beside the lake
dancing with grains of gold from the mines above.
We pinched ourselves. Was this your latest trick?
The day was so bright we must be crossing
the water still, in some crag-walking dream.

Sweating up the big scree boulders we met
goats. I memorised your eulogy. We rushed
up a jinksy little slab climb of closed
cracks called Expectancy, then abseiled
off a metal ring against the deadline
of your funeral. (Are you writing this?)
You'd have laughed at the three of us changing
in the carpark toilets. We heard you laughing
as we circled round the Sugar Loaf Mountain
searching, cursing, asking for the right church
which was the first church we had passed.

Poems and poignant pipes, words and weeping,
a fiddle and bright flowers sent you down.
In the quiet sunlight and open fields
by the mountain, the crowd could not leave,

could not come to believe that it was you
under that mound of wet Wicklow earth.
How the Irish understand the circle.
Exile and return. A tower, a round cross,
a ring of a hill. What you gave us was
Expectancy, a life that leaped circles,
as full of surprises as your death.

Fondue Strings
for Gill

A guitar strums
      out of an attic window
and the sky is in its last,
      palest blue of evening.
Everything has slowed
      here in our sultry street.
I slop along
      to post you a poem
about the alpinists
      you're not interested in.
Well, I thought maybe
      just getting mail
would be good.
      I wish I did not know
that beach restaurant
      you rang me from,
that breeze off the sea
      lifting your hair.
I have been hoovering
      your hairs from my car
and thinking if
      we were to part
I'd be finding those
      long, thin, strings
of fondue you can't
      break coming out
of my car seats forever.
      The hoover has given up
with them completely,
      and so have I.
You say, 'You're not
      very good on your own.'
I know, I give up
      too easily,
like your hair

apparently.
It accepts your absence
            and prefers my car
with a strong independence
            learned from your head.
You call it
            'emotional dependence',
my wanting to
            shorten the distance,
thinking of you
            whilst cleaning the car,
whilst climbing in France,
            even on a cold bivvi
before a big summit day,
            even whilst eating
the fondue of success,
            and wanting to come home
early before you fly
            for your sun-break.
Me, I still need
            those fondue strings,
even to call them
            'love'.

From Jack Scout Crag

We look out there over the lip
of the earth and see
only the beginning
of the sea's uplifted gift –
the alchemical drama
screened on our skin of sky.

Down here the sea's gone
out, cleansing the gut
of our gastric earth –
the infections of cities,
the urine of factories,
the additives of agriculture.

Down here the sea's gone,
leaving these alimentary
canals to shelduck and curlew
feeding under the living
wind-patterns of water,
the slow patterns of sand.

Out there the sea's coming
back as a long cascade
of white light washing in between
the nuclear ulcer of Heysham
Power Station and the gallstone
of Vickers at Barrow from which

one day submarine explosions will rupture our skin.

WHALE WATCHING
WITH A BOY AND A GOAT (1998)

Hunting the Dolmen of Haute Languedoc

I pause on the first bend
out of the village and study
the stillness deep in the gorge.
Only the martins move through it.

The last of the morning mists
of Haute Languedoc are fading fast
on horizon beyond horizon. Still
everything sleeps under the sun.

Cycling shirtless up the bends
where light passes through
the pale dry grassheads, I scan
shrubbed limestone pavement

for the lifted flat stone,
the old form, its gravity
defining the elements: sky
and earth held in balance.

Those who raised this old magic
in this high, wide place possessed
a certainty that still can
stagger me at first view.

My frail bicycle wheels spin
as I lay my machine to rest
and confront a stone culture
that must have also known

the ways of water, sun and wind
upon their white shellrock: that
the river dries back underground
differently each generation,

that the cave collapses and
the very rock is remnant –
there is no permanence.
But this is our certainty.

'Taylorgill Force, Seathwaite' by Ian Walton

And the more he looked
the more he heard only
that far fall of narrow light
where the whole sky's rain
was funnelled into a glittering
roar, the single iridescent voice
of the dark fell, its deep woods
and silent walls, until, still staring
and staring, there came out of the gloom
this nearer, frailer, higher sound
of water wearing its way through the land
as if lit by a last touch of sun
for barely a moment
before night closed upon
Taylorgill Force,
the sky cutting a mountain.

Inishmore

So finally, backs to the sea,
they walled themselves in,
here where good green earth
dreams a black jaw foaming,
its roar constant under the wind's edge.

Backs to the storms' salt spray
they rolled grey rocks into tight
chainmail, semi-circling themselves,
their potatoes, their goats,
their smoke-dark turf huts.

And next summer they started again,
rolling, levering, raising,
the outer circle confirming
their confidence here between
the weather and the walls.

So now, backs to the cosmos,
we remain between walls
and warming weather, musing
and musing on how to reverse
the outer circle we've made.

from Poland, October 1991

II
Why is No-one Jogging?

It is Sunday afternoon
at the allotments of Gliwice,
dug in between the main road
flowing constantly with cars
and the river flowing swiftly
with raw sewage towards
the tower blocks of the town.

I am jogging with GREENPEACE
on my vest towards the chimneys
beyond the town, beyond the park,
dark with big trees, grass uncut,
where few families are walking.

I am jogging down the ash road
past the allotments' wire fences
and high gates. Hard to tell
how many families are here
among the fruit trees and huts,
a private home, a chimneyed house
you can call your own.

This is the family heirloom:
subsistence, retreat, but not
to turn potatoes out of earth
that is poisoned by pollution.
Resistance is in flowers!
Answer communism with cacti
in your greenhouse! Whilst they can
pickle fungi from the fields,
or harvest nuts from the woods,
they cannot eat the apple of bad air,
the fruit of their father's tree.

But here they could talk
without being overheard,
exchange jokes and seeds
of a green opposition
that in those days swelled
to things you could eat.

It is Sunday afternoon
at the allotments of Gliwice
and democracy has flowered
into so many heads
that no-one knows how many.
Several are Green
and hold the seeds
of unemployment, they are saying
here in the second homes.

from Poland, October 1991

V
Return Journey

An icy moon is tipped above
the first glow of dawn
as the frosted towns drift by:
Gliwice, Zabze, Katowice.
At each station the faces
of the old ones fill with tears
as they wave off furiously
their children and their children
after the All Saints Day visit.

Yesterday the old ones scrubbed
the tombs, polished the marble
of the graves of their parents
while the roads of the nation
throbbed, the railway lines pulsed
with the pull of family blood
back to the burial grounds.

After so many borders redrawn,
repatriation, insurrection,
and now the latest liberation,
the Poles returned last night
to the land of the dead.
Every cemetery was lit
by thousands of candles
clustered on the glinting tombs.

Amongst the heavy odour of
chrysanthemums in armfuls
arranged earlier on every grave,
the nation walked with its past,

stared together at the life
of the last generation,
revisited each year at
what the communists renamed
'The Festival of the Dead'
and can now be reclaimed
as 'All Hallows E'en'.

Not Nature Writing

for Gill

I

Tentless, stoveless, mapless
we leave for three days,
Dave Mazel and me, lighting out
into the Bitterroot Mountains
like naive, excited kids
following a tale of a trail
Dave had heard back by the river
in Missoula where Barry Lopez
had read like a sage. I heard
the bugs are bad out there.

But, hey, we have bread
and cheese, salami and wine.
There's blue behind those
Montana thunderheads and water
springs clear from mossy holes
beside the path we finally lose
at a lake. We search around and return.
'How about we balance
across the log dam?' Dave's words
are better than Nature Writing.

There's a faint trail on the far
side and a view of a peak
like a layered iced cake.
'Wouldn't that make a noble
objective?' Dave has an ice-axe
and a language to match.
'Bushwhacking' is the only word
for our illiterate attempts to find
animal trails that read rock shelves
into a high basin, a grassy glade.

II

Now, I could tell you about
the lightening storm that night,
about my neolithic snow daggers,
a sudden wilderness of peaks,
the bull moose grazing through
his evening glade's willow fringe,
but even those ferocious
all dancing, all biting bugs
pale beside that moment when
I pulled from my sleeping bag

your shirt, that sleeveless blue
gingham thing that seemed
too small, frail, far away.
Even travelling light
into a wild, still, retreat
you were there, at the back
of my head as I looked out
and learned how to be attentive,
how to listen both ways,
get up and get down the mountain.

Whale Watching with a Boy and a Goat

'Check out the wild flowers', he says.
I bend over an orange trumpet vibrating
towards the sun from thin gravel and grass.
The goat, its lead slipped, does the same.
'Hey, a red tailed hawk!' Checking us out,
tilting, turning, the bird wobbles its spread
tail glowing like sunlit stained glass.

Coming over a rise the boy, trotting goat,
and I suddenly hear the ocean's deep throated
pounding in from Asia onto this Californian shore.
I am led down onto his headland like a child.
This boy of twelve is my guide to whale watching.
'Here's a coyote scat – that's a scientific word
for poop.' I'm to look south for a spout, then
for another close behind, mother and calf passing
Shark Bay to summer, if they make it, off Canada.

My guide was off school sick, but before I set out
he came over O.K., needed fresh air. He wrestles
with the goat above the yellow foam-fingered bay
while I scan the green sea for a dark cruising
shape close in, or a fabled fountain far out.
The day passes like they do in California. Mist
closes over the hills up the coast. The sea breeze
chills. All the small flowers have been seen. Coffee
calls, back at his house in the woods. We head home.

The boy keeps waving me ahead. He slows to slower
than sauntering. A mile short of home I decide
he is ill, run ahead for his mother and the van
for the boy and the goat. He'd had the shits bad
and pooped his pants, guiding a stranger and all,
who had not even seen a whale. His mother smiled.
Next day I watched again: one spout, then another.

Pat's Webbed Feet

They said I lived on water when I was young.
Leaving my land life behind after the bell
I slipped my mooring and found my proper balance
under sail. I could read the wind across
a sheet of water, knew the maze of reedbeds,
dykes and reaches. The Broads, empty at evening,
were my Looking-Glass Land. An hour or two out
I'd try to lose myself, set the sail, slip down
into the bottom of the boat and stare at sky,
listen to the lap of water on the clinkers,
the courting cries of wildfowl, until a nudge
of mudbank told me it was time to tie up
and find the nearest church. A tower drew me to it
like a mast. But I'd want to leave my mark. Always
I'd sign the book then walk away to water once again,
until the summer of my sixteenth year. I'd drifted,
drifted into this church and sat too long.
It was getting dark. I found the fat leather
visitors' book, opened it and suddenly saw the flat
black body of a frog, its webbed feet spread
on the white page. That was the summer I sold the boat
and met a boy who had an old black dreamy car.
We found some lanes you wouldn't know were there.

The Single Falling Stone

i.m. Paul Nunn

Whenever I take the longest drive north
and west at Whitsun I think of Nunn other
than a name that echoes through the guidebook
like his laugh, the indoor bagpipes
of the climbing village, slightly embarrassing,
needing all the space of Peakland moors,
Sutherland, the Karakoram: 'as the mountain valleys
open up one feels that one is coming home.'

Outlandish, like those obscure scraps
of facts he'd pin you down with while
he built a theory between one pint and the next
he'd always offer anyone at hand. Such hands
you'd think grasped summits annually, yet
how often he'd return empty handed home
from home. 'We had no commitments, except
to ourselves, and they were satisfied.'

He'd lost friends to the single falling stone,
the sudden moment of snow slide, serac crack
we must struggle to accept. 'Some day soon
some must fall. It was a case of grinning
and ignoring them.' Out here, where sea
and mountains meet, where the sky's big-hearted,
something is missing and present between sun
and showers in his 'far far away land'.

What Bashō Could Say in Three Lines

In the stillness of North Carolina's Linville Gorge
the river's roar rises to the walls of Shortoff Mountain.
It is always there, cutting, grading, taking and giving
to Lake James. Only the bear hunters know it closely
in this cold season. I hear it when I look down, turning
slowly on the rope-end like a chrysalis on a thread under
the overhang I've finally fallen off. I rest, let the river in,
then turn my mind to ways of butterflying out of this
dead-end. Lowered to the crack off left and I'm flying
on a different course, fumbling to find a state of grace.

How our lives are measured by love songs as we travel.
In the truck, country singers try for images of 'flowing
like a river from the mountains to the sea'. They know
their clichés give a playful sense of control. They sing,
'How can I miss you if you won't go away?'
Rednecks ready to redefine a dead-end, moving on
without that butterfly stuff. I've moved away a while
and I miss you. It's your birthday and I'm a continent away.
You call back when you've opened my present, a mountain
painting. No need for us to say 'I love you' and we don't.

A friend picks me up to drive to dinner at the home
of a woman who hugs me as I hold out my hand.
On the drive home suddenly my friend is saying,
'to hear the words "I love you" from your life's partner –
that's what I haven't heard for two years, since
my wife died. It's hard, you know?' And I find myself
struggling to respond, wanting to say something
of what a mountain learns from a cold river, what a river gives
to a humbled mountain, how the bear senses flash floods
and how the river finds its way onward, onward, onward.

THE UNRELIABLE MUSHROOMS:
NEW POEMS

English Earth Warriors

I The Bag Man

Remember Ed Abbey, that old American
  anarchist conservationist?
Loved the dirt of the desert, the silence of slickrock,
  tossed his beer cans out of the car
Driving highways through Arches, all of Arizona.
  Invented The Monkey Wrench Gang,
Railed against dams, but littered the verge with his cans
  where the wilderness had been lost.

That's Abbey's icon, a man's beer can asking the question,
  'Do you give a damn for the desert?'
I prefer plastic. I play the Greek shepherd like
  Polystyrene, Polyvinyl.
And I work at night. Better for the alchemy
  of polymers out in the fields.
Helped by high winds I can transform a hedge,
  a tree, into a thing of beauty.

It takes a French philosopher to see it clearly:
  'It's the first magical substance
To consent to be prosaic.' Hey, plastic
  brings out the plastic in nature.
Carrier bags fruit from the tree's form, shepherds' feed bags
  define the forgotten corners of fields.
That black wrinkly haybale wrapper, my favourite,
  pierced and stretched, becomes the hedge.

I, too, work the motorway verges of England –
  no need to wait for the full moon.
Factories can give fine streamers through bushes.
  Wind can become plastic like smoke.
I've gone beyond Roland Barthes and Ed Abbey:
  my artistry reveals nature,
Its living form shaped by the artifice of decay.
  And they'll never find out that it's me.

75

II The Ball Man

Over the years, walking the dog, I have got to know
        the awkward places: the bottoms
Of bushes, a thicket at the foot of a slope,
        where gravity drags everything
Finally, into the earth's secret folds and holes:
        the underworld of undergrowth.
I trained the dog to retrieve from streams. I'd throw
        a stone. He'd return with a golf ball.

Of course, there is the frisson of not being sure,
        absolutely, that one is lost.
Between my outstretched fingers and my pocket
        I awaited the cry from behind.
When it came I didn't expect the relief.
        I buried him, recruited for
My mission on behalf of the land underneath
        this manicured, painted, play space.

The real skill is to use wedging and balance
        to execute the idea.
Against the perfection of shape, imperfection
        of texture is helpful to me.
The first one I placed was in the fork of a tree.
        The trickiest challenge I set
Myself was the highest windowsill of the clubhouse.
        The funniest, a thrush's nest.

Or, no, perhaps it was the one I half buried
        in the top corner of a green.
Lately I've found a new kind of provocation
        based on the unnatural form
Of a triangle: three balls balanced on their tees
        On some greens. They find two and know
There's another somewhere, hidden, like that guy.
        I know some very awkward places.

III The Nestbox Nurses

I'm not sure how we got started. Pub talk probably.
    'But what do we do?' Gary said.
I remember that. 'We pay Greenpeace to do it.'
    It was true for three of us on our shift.
And when we started those mid-week walks Clare said,
    'Why do we need all those road signs –
North Lees Estate. Sheep. 40mph. Slow lambs crossing?'
    Gary had heard of 'The Cairnmakers'.

So we made these signs, the pictures: birds, rain, rocks, rain –
    Clare was good at that – and the words:
Approaching Burbage. Closer to Burbage. Burbage.
    and hammered them in for Sunday
Like Scottish 'Cairnmakers' deluding English walkers.
    The false footpath posts were easier,
Criss-crossing Burbage bog. We vetoed Gary's stile,
    Alone at the fence-less centre.

Up on Ward 27 we giggle a lot,
    after we've comforted and calmed
Like the moors do for us. But it isn't us who
    are putting parking meters
Out there and building boardwalks across wet bogs.
    And we aren't mink liberators,
Or those who take pity on big cat pets, release
    At night a puma on Exmoor.

We talk, as we walk, about nestboxes in woods –
    Who are they for? Birds, or humans?
Should they be in wild woods? One shift last week
    Clare held up a bandage box and said,
'All this needs is brown paint like wood, a cut hole and
    glued tab.' Gary said, 'Leave the ladder
To me. Friday night. Derwent Woods. We'll nail one on
    every tree. We're Nestbox Nurses. See?'

IV The Land Artist

Yes, they get grants, Andy Goldsworthy, Richard Long.
　　　　　The Tate wants them, much as they hate
Walking the Tate, making what should be in deserts, moors.
　　　　　But they must bring it back framed by
Book, video, photo or the gallery floor.
　　　　　Yes, they betray their locations.
Because, see, their work is not witnessed in place,
　　　　　a witness to place. It's for them.

I, too, read the terrain, from the roads all around
　　　　　and learn the stresses of stanchions
And bolts, the aerodynamics of an angel.
　　　　　The poor tenants of horizons
Are dour, even bolshie, but not too hard to 'bribe'
　　　　　when they know what I know about
Their grant applications. I hack into their files.
　　　　　They shrug and I work without grants.

'Honeypots', the Park Planners call them, the places
　　　　　they've given up to ice-cream vans
Where they put the car-park, and probably the lake –
　　　　　well, the pre-Planners – engineers
Like me and the makers of those huge roadside bulls
　　　　　in Spain, balls withstanding all winds.
They're ironic land-art, see, selling sherry made
　　　　　for England back to the Spanish.

So I got to thinking, 'Where will it end?' I can
　　　　　show them with a week's workshop graft
And a day in the right place, the farmer onside:
　　　　　the Forest of Bowland, South Downs,
Tryfan summit, Stanage High Neb, Upper Swaledale –
　　　　　at least a week of paperwork
Before it comes down, a week of passing drivers
　　　　　saying, 'An ice-cream van, up there?'

A Milesian Encounter with a Spider in Spain

How long had I been sitting here
on the sunny doorstep of the street
before this spider came to visit my book?

It arrived by a horizontal line from the doorpost
I suddenly realised was another street I was part of,
actually structured into. And me thinking

I was made immaterial by the old lady in black
next door who talks to her cat, or the street,
here, above a scree of pale orange roof-tiles.

Beyond my two metre wide street and a low wall
are old TV aerials and the odd solar panel
in waves of tiles, the new yellow builders' crane

and ancient back-breaking terraces tracing
contours round hills to the sea in a V.
Above, mountains shadow changes under clouds.

And this spider traverses in on the street wind
to feel my turned pages with twin feelers
on horizontal antennae from its small black head.

I watch it reading, delicately, slightly open pages.
It decides to turn around, with its four legs,
its yellow body and go over the back, but

not for long. It's soon up on the page corners
and considering, like me, its next thought.
Well, we wait for each other, looking, sensing

what is happening, the nature of where we are.
I could blow it off, get on with my book, but
it blows me off, bunching all its legs, upside

down on another street back to the geranium
in the doorstep tub and I focus back to
Keith Sagar's words about that spider-watcher

Ted Hughes, contemplating his conclusion: 'Perhaps
the best we can hope for is that our civilisation
will end like any other, seeming no more than a nightmare...'

Haikus for a Kaki Tree

*Haikus for the planting of a Kaki tree, a sapling taken
from a tree that survived Nagasaki.
The Earth Centre, Doncaster, 1999.*

Out of our horror
      nature grew this frail sign to
         improve our nature.

Here young voices rise
      like kites to plant this grafted
         old barometer.

At a Pass in the Mountain

Consider the scree:
its black wet blocks
supporting each other

in freefall, the mountain
constantly on the move
under its solid brow.

Between the last eight-thousander
and the first heart-attack
I have time to reflect,

says Messner, as though
the word 'menopause'
is as simple as 'scree'.

Consider the crag:
a community of roots,
interlocking riches of love

too needy to countenance
competition up there,
holding on to each other.

The very stones seem
talkative, sympathetic,
says Muir on Cathedral Peak,

hearing only his own
heartbeat in every crystal,
not his death in the desert.

Consider the silver
fall-pipe of water, drinking
the summit, throating the crag,

sluicing the scree
into the bowl of the river,
storm-scoured with gravity.

The land carries the stories
that can give us the knowledge
of how to behave there,

says David Abram, not saying
how to read this scree, this crag
and these waterfalls ageing the Pass.

Makryalos, Crete

Red day and white night:
      thrusting trumpets; perfumed bells.
          Hibiscus; jasmine.

Long spear poised above
      harbour wall, blue lycra sheen
          in sun: kingfisher.

Above the olives
      a spring. Above this a church.
          Which is blessing which?

The Day Ted Hughes Died

I

I drove up out of town to jog as usual
for a Thursday lunchtime, sidestepping
on autopilot those familiar puddles
in the Burbage Green Drive, thinking,

Moor. Stone. Sky. He taught me
what these words mean. Look. This,
I said to myself, is moor. It lives
for this emptiness. Look at that grit,

God's own rock, his way of saying
Stone. Listen to that sky, those epic dramas
played out above the heads of most of us:
the tragedy of Mother Earth and the child

who rejects her. It was all so young,
so fresh from the furnace, this free gift
with hidden costs, strangely bright
with its own light for late October.

II

And what part of me had died
that day when the call came
from the local radio station, low-key,
like a policeman, assuming intimacy:
'I've got some bad news for you ...
Can you come in and do an interview?'
I ran, like Ted had. He chose life,
thinking to outface death by deflection

with all the passion and pain
learned of woman – survival, wit,
the vitality of humour, the almost
crushing grief of unchosen partings.

What parts of me will I muster
to face that final standing-off,
bodily resources shrinking, saying,
and having to mean it: 'This also is life?'

III

A November bat had hovered over the coffin
in the church next to his thatched house
that shared the famous moon-holding elm tree.
'That's Ted', Olwyn had murmured to a friend.

In Westminster Abbey, after the turn of a winter,
men wanted to hint quietly to each other
how we had cried at the sound of his voice
echoing deeply, softly, *Fear no more*

the heat o' the sun, Nor the furious winter's rages.
How that voice, filling the arched air
of the Abbey, had surprised us with tears.
But we said, 'That was too much.'

'Caught me off-guard.' 'That was it.'
We had not learned the reasoning of rivers,
the cleansing of a devout drench.
We walked away from the Abbey knowing

that a great bird had landed here,
had strangely filled us up, and was gone.

IV

i.m. Fred Rue Jacobs
Dunnerdale, 18 September 1999

I'm writing in the last house up a valley
in the Lake District and Fred is here
at midnight saying, 'Hey, life ain't so bad!'
and 'I've had the cancer all these years, but
hey, I'm a success!' as I ignore my own
mortality in pursuit of the natural wonders
in those books, the bull backlit by moonlight
in the mist of the meadow I just walked through.
I only saw it when I looked back. Looking back,

I did not expect to meet Fred in Cairo,
but when I went for breakfast on the top floor
of the hotel there he was drinking beer,
waiting for people to appear, ignoring
brilliant parakeets below. At dinner over here
his gift of laughter was a little too loud
for English ears. For breakfast in California
Fred's fridge was always stocked with nuts
and beer. Just nuts and beer. 'Perfect!'

When I go to the door, peer into the dark
across the still meadow towards the woods,
I hear the owls of the valley laughing, echoing,
and recall Ted's dedications in those books
in Fred's Bakersfield 'shrine': *Only an owl*
knows the worth of an owl. Fred was a man
worthy of his collection, as I think Ted knew
when he simply wrote, *This one's for Fred,*
living his death with such knowing fun.

Lake Norman, North Carolina
for Helena and the Winter family

*There comes a time when they won't be hugged
because they're hugging someone else.*

Easy, in the quickening bustle of morning's birds,
to lose the nocturnes of last night: the teenagers
in a circle on the floor sharing stories of dreams

and little Arley holding my hand along the boat dock
walking out to see how water held the floating light
as woods and land were black with night already,

the good omen of the Great Blue Heron, huge, right
overhead, rowing homeward on deep wings, then
ripples through the water nosing toward the boathouse,

how we whispered our way back to ask what
it could be. No sooner had 'Muskrat' been said
than we turned to see an orange moon pulling

out of far woods, spilling light across the lake
right up to our feet where we all were gathered
to accept the gift of this place, holding hands.

***

Dawn, an orange smudge behind thick mist
that gave this three-stemmed tree solidity.
The lake, white as the air around these strange

floating struts that make an empty boathouse,
until the lake surface smokes away above
rippled shallows and wind draws the curtain

to show, in this brightest light, a tiny marvel
moving with the morning's sharp energy:
Brown-headed Nuthatches feeding young

in a hole hidden atop a bowing snag of the tree.
They bring caterpillars that now are leaving
their sun-warmed silk sacks, thinking they're fledged.

Upon the Dangers of Climbing
Castle Rock of Triermain

Butterlip How?
Strickland, Roger,
Honister.

Pass the Fawcett
Forest Docker
Longsleddale,
Sleddale,
Sleddale -

Whin Fell,
Birk.
Greyrigg
and Green Gills.

Flew Scar.

Honister.

Ill Bell,
Lawyer's Brow,
Wrynose
and Aikrigg
in Lord's Seat,

but Goodham Scales
and Hipshow,
Summerhow.

No Spital Fowl Ing.
No Yoadpot.
No Toadpool.

Just a Kentrigg
and a Mozergh House.

Honister.

The Charcoal Burner's Tale

Once upon a time there was a charcoal burner
who worked at his sooty furnace in the olive groves
beside the dry river bed beyond the cement factory.

His chickens scraped at the woodland floor
free of fear, for there are no foxes on Crete,
only Beech Martins and hungry Albanians.

Towards him, one day, there walked a woman
up out of the river gorge, white as a gull, smiling
from under her cap, binoculars swinging between

her breasts, her hair pale as straw, shorts, thick legs
and her man behind her, shorts, thick neck,
black binoculars in his white, thin hands.

'Germans', the charcoal burner said to his hens.
'They're everywhere now, even out of season'.
But he put his father's curses aside and spoke

in welcome, as the habit of his country required
of the surprise meeting of strangers in the woods
that were his workplace in the heat of summer.

His charcoal went to these Germans and their beach
barbecues at bars beside the turtle nesting places
his father had showed him at a dawn of frenzy –

tiny turtles sand-swimming towards the sea, and gulls
feasting on the soft shore of death and growing up.
Here in the woods, the filthy charcoal burner smiled

his toothless smile and spoke his words of welcome
with vigorous gestures, laughing at their whiteness.
But his guests kept moving, unease in their smiles, fear

for some reason, behind their eyes, their fathers' eyes
he supposed, though he had spoken with no more
than his usual wit, for which he was well known.

Eclipse at Mochlos

Dirt, a trowel, a small brush
and a searing sun.
I was squatting in a corner
where the low stone walls
of what was once a room
offered no relief.
Like my carefully conserved
water, I was getting warmer
and trying to last only until
the afternoon return boat
summoned by the bell
of a simple unused church.
It was a barren, small island:
swimming distance from the village,
not good enough for goats.

Layers of dirt, stirred to dust
by the trowel's point, were my focus,
poking at the edges of small stones
and prising them up to cast aside
for the sieve-shaker's examination,
until brushed curves became a handle
on a fragment of a vessel.
I stood up and passed my finger
through a circle no finger had closed
for four thousand years, looked
round in the eerie dimness for
the others. They were gathered
at the sieve, taking it in turns,
through eight layers of sunglasses,
to peer skywards at some discovery.

Cretan Post-Pastoral

Each day's end the mountain closes the sun –
watch it go until that glow remaining shows
the solitary tree that before you could not see.

In the hills where they harvest honey
a huge mirror is being built in a bowl to throw
the sun at 800 degrees towards a solitary turbine.

In a hollow in the barren hills windmills
water fields of green. Below, watermills
in spring made flour for solitary ovens.

This is an island without trains
to which we come by planes and rent
a car for the pull up a solitary mountain

where there's a church perched on the peak
against all ills. But world oil will spill its last
drop and stop even a solitary pastoral journey

and we'll learn again to mill and bake,
hunkered down in our own land, learning
from a solitary tree that before we could not see.

'The Forest Fire'
Piero di Cosimo (1505)
September 2001

They came tumbling out. Lumpen,
It must have felt, an unreal slow
Motion of raw animal energy.
Some courtesies were observed
And, later, became famous heroisms:
The lion turning back towards the deer.
But mostly it was boars, bears and bulls
Each fleeing their familiar pastoral patch.
They came with themselves only.
It was all they had against the heat,
The furnace that transformed them,
Once they'd realised, too late, that they'd
Never be the same. They were changing
In their heads, between human and beast.
They weren't what they were when they started
Their bright morning's work in that tall forest.
The fast birds easily outstripped them, although
There were those flapping on high branches
About to attempt unfamiliar flight.
'All awkwardness and confusion, an allegory
Of evolution,' commentators would say
Of the vivid oils on four long poplar panels
Disturbing the civilized quiet of the Ashmolean.
And still nobody quite knows what it means.

For Sybil on Her Eightieth Birthday

The moon may have lost its mystery –
Visited, footprinted, buggy-abandoned,
But it is still a fine thing to find hanging
Above dark mountains, a tiered town,

A roof-terrace armchair on a warm night
In Spain where you suddenly recall the mystery
Of the crystal set your father built on its
Board of blue that came with the kit.

Now you need a modem to email grandchildren
In Munich and London, putting the typing skills
That liberated, briefly, your female generation
To the leisure use of our computer age.

This very morning I passed a little girl
Dressed in florescent green, arms outstretched,
Flying, banking and tilting along before her parents
And I needed some crystal ball to fastforward

To see how, at eighty, she would communicate
With her grandchildren, slowly learn from them
Their technologies, watch them running ahead
In their brilliant bodies, see them fly.

'Fall to Rise' by Russell Mills, 1997

Collage, earth, pigments, acrylics,
oils, metal, leaf, in box.

I was drawn across the gallery
to a bleached wooden toolbox
mounted on the wall. It held a gold leaf:
half gold, half the filaments of decay
glued on a square of polaroid film.

If I had such a box to give you
what would I put on that polaroid?
Your first fall onto the beach towel
to unwrap white flesh and wade in,
clean as a fish, buttocks, waist, breasts

turning into floating sunlit gold
as you swim away, away, away.
In my future polaroids there's only
shape-shifting, not decay: golden
beaches we'll cross on walking-sticks.

But in the margin between the inner box
and the outer box are torn, curling leaves
of text: Goldsmith's *Natural History*,
first edition, but torn into falling scraps,
said the artist, because it's full of errors.

If I had such a marginal gap,
I would give you this natural history –
four young swallows fallen
on first wing-flaps from their mud nest
on the light bulb of the campsite toilet block

to rise upon the ceramic cistern rim –
first flight before the haul to Africa.
It's September. Summer's beaches fade
into the photographs and like the leaves
we both must face the fall to rise.

The Unreliable Mushrooms

Alone, I'm quartering our mushroom field again.
It can't decide to rain.
From Germany, 'It's hot',
you say. Here, harebells hang on in the long grasses
and sheep dung
and thistles.
You'd know if I'm too early. White nipples push
through earth
below the path.
On the upper slope the deadly red are emerging
for their annual
Oktoberfest.

I zig-zag down the pasture and find
fawn-speckled domes.
To pluck them
is the softest touch, and their delicate gills,
white sprays
of fungi fugues,
sing from a centre outwards to reach
perfected form.
I'm uncertain
what I'm holding here. I need the book.
I wish you'd ring.
I can't find it,
quartering the fields of books at home.

You had it last.
I can't cook
these until you call. Why have I no confidence
in my own
mushrooms?
I remember them, recognise them from
last year
I think.
We fried them, together, with garlic, I think.
Why don't you call?
I need our book.
Then I can start my own wild mushroom omelette.